09/2009

Yiddish Yoga

Yiddish Yoga

Ruthie's Adventures in Love, Loss, and the Lotus Position

Lisa Grunberger

Illustrations by Art Glazer

NEWMARKET PRESS
NEW YORK

To my mother, Rachel Grunberger (1925–1992)

FIRST EDITION

ISBN: 978-1-55704-835-6
10 9 8 7 6 5 4 3 2 1

Library of Congress Cataloging-in-Publication Data
Grunberger, Lisa.
  Yiddish yoga : Ruthie's adventures in love, loss, and the lotus position / Lisa Grunberger, Ph.D. — 1st ed.
    p. cm.
  ISBN 978-1-55704-835-6 (alk. paper)
  1. Grandmothers—Fiction. 2. Yoga—Fiction. 3. Widows—New York (State)—New York—Fiction. I. Title.
  PS3607.R754Y53 2009
  813'.6—dc22   2009017796

Designed by Kris Tobiassen

Manufactured in the United States of America.

www.newmarketpress.com

Stephie's Gift of Yoga

Dear Bubby,

We either meet at *simchas*, like Uncle David's birthday last year, or at funerals, like Zayde's.

I miss the in-between time with you, Bubby. Remember the Sundays when we'd play backgammon all day, and you would let me have milky coffee like a grown-up?

I know you don't like gifts or compliments, and I know you will resist this like the plague, but—are you sitting down?—I'm sending you a year's gift of yoga! It's so convenient, too—right down the block from your apartment!

Yoga will keep you young and balanced so you can live *bis hundert un tsvantsik*—till 120—and be a great-grandmother (no, I'm not pregnant). I know you are strong, Bubby, but I think yoga will help you grieve. This is not a cult, I promise! I do it every day since Mark and I broke up, and have never felt better.

I hope we will share a plate of your delicious potato *latkes,* topped with sour cream and applesauce, for Hanukkah . . . and go to yoga class.

We will celebrate the "in-between" days because, as John Lennon* said, "Life is what happens when you're busy making other plans."

At the risk of guilting you into going, these yoga classes cost me a small fortune.

I love you.

Hugs and kisses,
Your granddaughter,

Stephie

*He's the one who wrote *Imagine*, not Paul McCartney, who was married to Linda until she died. He recently married a woman who divorced him and got over a $30 million settlement. I know, I know, when the time comes, I should insist on a pre-nup. "Pre-nup or no-nip" is your motto.

The Cost of Dreams

Last week, I had a dream that I was floating on a giant flying carpet—a gift certificate for a year of free yoga classes!

I must say it was very relaxing, just drifting through the heavens. Kind of like Miami Beach meets Calcutta.

There were rabbis and yogis, and they all had long hair and flowing robes. I kept crying out to the clouds, "I'm the Hippy Bubby Extraordinaire from Manhattan!"

But I woke up in a panic—*Oy vey iz mir!* Oh, woe is me!—the cost of all this drifting and dreaming. My poor granddaughter, Stephanie, *meine maidela*, spent a small fortune on these yoga classes for her Bubby.

"To help you grieve, Bubby. It will be healing for you."

When I got up, I went straight to the yoga center—I haven't moved so fast since I *loifed* to Loehmann's fifty percent, post-holiday, red tag sale!

Ruthie Goes to Yoga

My first yoga class! The teacher is so young! Uch!
He wants us to "set an intention."

What can this mean? *Intention?*

My intention is to have a pastrami sandwich at
Katz's Deli on Houston.

Breathe in, breathe out, breathe in, breathe out. He
keeps repeating it like we can't hear him. What am
I, a human respirator?

For twenty minutes we sit in what we used to call
"Indian style." After a while my hips are so numb, I
think I need a Percodan.

All this focus on breathing makes me light-headed.

What a *nudnik* the teacher is.

Schvitzing and Noshing in Yoga Class

At the Yoga Center I was famished and looked around for a *nosh*. I asked one of the staff (the one with the nose ring, I would say, but this would not distinguish her from all the others), "Excuse me, where's your snack bar?"

She looked at me with eyes more glazed than a Krispy Kreme doughnut.

"You shouldn't eat right before class," she advised. "Sip the air—it's composed of seventy percent water, like your body."

No wonder they're all emaciated: there's no food, the heat's up to a hundred degrees—and they're sipping air!

What to Wear to Yoga Class?

The girl at the front desk had said to dress
comfortably. I had no idea what to wear to this
meshuga class. There was no way I was going to wear
thongs!

So I pulled out my old blue-and-white Adidas
velour sweatsuit. Harry (may he rest in peace)
bought it for me at Macy's for our trip to Israel a
lifetime ago. When I put it on, I swear I could hear
him whistle at me.

It never fails to make me blush.

Props

In this class, there are all kinds of props. Purple bricks and Guatemalan blankets (I wondered when they were last washed) and straps. Straps? Did I wander into an S & M class?

So I'm on my purple yoga mat and my dirty Guatemalan blanket with my straps, and I begin to breathe. In and out, in and out—I'm starting to hyperventilate!

SAT YAM LUPINSKY, A MENSCH

My instructor is called Sat Yam, but with a *ponem* like his, I did some reconnoitering and found out his name is Schmuel Lupinsky. I'll call him Sammy. So young he is. Very tall, like my Harry, and quite handsome (if he would shave the beard). Could Sammy be one of those Jewish-Buddhists—a Jew-Bu—that Stephanie told me about? Stephanie said the Buddhists, like the Jews, want to end suffering, and heal all sentient beings. Jews call it *tikkun ha-olam*—to save the world. I'm confused—wouldn't he technically be a Hindu-Jew, or a Hin-Jew, since yoga comes from the Hindu tradition? Oy, so many new things to absorb in yoga!

Sammy is certainly repairing me—such a *mensch* he is, always bringing me blocks and straps and extra blankets. He turns the music down low and speaks extra loud so I can hear everything.

What *rachmones*—compassion—this man has, and to a virtual stranger yet.

TOUCHY-FEELY YOGA—NOT!

Sammy is so respectful—he always asks whether it's okay if he adjusts our postures. He says he doesn't want to violate a person's personal space. Violate, please! Sometimes, I must confess, I do the postures wrong intentionally. *Bubeleh*, adjust, adjust!

Living in New York City, it's hard *not* to violate someone's space. People aren't so touchy-feely in the Big Apple—they are pushy-stealy!

Injuries

Sammy asks the class, "Are there any injuries I should be aware of before we begin?"

I raise my hand and begin telling him about my various ailments: my left hip and the sciatica; the pinched nerve in my neck; my bunions (of course); my acid reflux, which could burn a hole in these Guatemalan blankets.

Another student cuts me off, sharing with the whole class that I'm giving her a headache.

Yoga Adjustments for a Widow

When I was younger, I was a looker. A fiery redhead, svelte, with a big bosom. Let's just say I was never at a loss for attention from men. My sister Pearl always said so. These days, we barely speak. *We* need *tikkun ha-olam,* but that's an adjustment I'm not quite ready for.

Now that Harry's gone, I miss human touch the most.

So when Sammy touches me in, say, Downward Dog Pose, such a *mitzvah!* I'm *kvelling,* happy to be touched.

Dhyāna: Meditating

Sammy says, "If you find yourself thinking, just say, 'Thinking, thinking,' and return to your breath."

I take the liberty of modifying this. When I find myself thinking, I say, "Valium, thank you, valium, thank you." My new *mantra*.

Kapalabhati—Who?

Today we learned *kapalabhati* breathing. *Kapala*
means "skull" in Sanskrit. You know how I
remember it? In Yiddish *kepeleh* means "little head."

Bhati means "that which brings lightness." With all
this deep breathing, my *kepeleh* is light.

I don't know about the lightness. I'm 150 pounds
zaftig!

Adho Mukha Svanasana: Downward Dog

Who says you can't teach an old dog new tricks?

Sammy says my Downward Dog looks good. Not bad for a seventy-two-year-old grandmother! Should I wag my tail?

I was feeling flirty.

KIRTAN: DEVOTIONAL CHANTING

They hand out chant sheets with the words printed out phonetically. May as well be Hebrew. *Om Nama Shivaya, Om Nama Shivaya.*

Oy veya, vaya, potato knish, maya, gefilte fish, kugel-mish, B'nai B'rith.

San-yish. Yidd-skrit. Sammy says that the most pleasing sound to God is laughter.

Simhasana: Lion Roar

We are instructed to mime a lion's claws and roar!
Supposed to be cathartic. Good to relieve jaw
tension, which many urban people suffer from.

It sounds like Primal Scream Therapy.

I just hope they're not piping in any brainwashing
material through the music.

I'm keeping an open mind. It's just that I'm from
the old school—a little cod-liver oil, some Jack
LaLanne, a morning constitutional, and I'm raring
to go.

Suddenly I'm a lioness, with a blood-red manicure.

CULTS

I hope this is not some kind of Hare Krishna cult, but you never know. Ruth Levine's youngest daughter, Cheryl, got involved with them, right on her college campus. It cost her parents thousands of dollars to deprogram her. And the worry—the worry alone would do me in.

However, I wouldn't mind being deprogrammed from ice cream. Particularly Ben and Jerry's Instant Marshmallow, Chocolate-Covered Pretzel, Peanut Butter Karma!

On Stiffness, Humor, and Grief

Grief can make you very stiff. Sammy closes class each time by saying, "Yoga gives us flexibility of body and mind."

P.S. I wonder if flexibility can erase grief. Smooth out its rough edges.

THE MONKEY MIND

I learned a delightful new term that comes from Buddhism: *monkey mind.* This is a metaphor of how jumpy and restless the mind often is. Through yoga and these moving meditations, we are supposed to settle the monkey down.

My monkey mind wants to know: Who, other than *meshugana* artists and the unemployed, can do yoga in the middle of the afternoon?

But King Solomon said there is a time for everything. A time for yoga, a time for Ruthie.

Yoga in the Details: Mudras

In the 8 a.m. Gentle Yoga Class, Sammy says God is in the big toe.

The thumb symbolizes *Brahman*, which is the divinity that unites us all. If you're like my agnostic friend Flora, you'll call it *eppes*, something like energy, the mystery.

The index finger represents the ego, so when we join the thumb and the index finger, this creates a hand gesture, or *mudra,* that reminds us to be humble.

Fat chance!

Whenever we bow forward in *uttanasana*, we bow in humility. I personally like the feeling of hanging upside down.

Plus, I get extra close to my toes—to check to see if it's time for a humble pedicure.

Surya Namaskar: Sun Salutes

During our Sun Salutes this morning, with the autumn rays pouring through the blinds, Sammy says we are saluting "old" light, a star, in delayed time.

It's a lot like memory, this humble salute.

When I honor my Harry in memory, I see him again, my old star.

Yoga of Klezmer

I have to confess that the music they play during
yoga puts me to sleep. This New Age music sounds
more like elevator music. I want something I can
move to, something uplifting. So when Sammy
played Louis Armstrong in class one day, I thought I
was going to *plotz*—just burst!

During *savasana,* the final meditation, I thought
I was either dreaming or dying when I heard the
quiet cry of a violin—Sammy was playing *klezmer*
music! On Sundays, my father would play his violin,
and my mother and I would dance around our small
living room.

When class was over, Sammy gave me the CD—he said it was a gift for being so committed to my practice. "You've come such a long way, Ruthie. You inspire me to keep moving."

I'm not a sentimental person, but I stood up on my toes and blew him a kiss.

NATARAJASANA: DANCING SHIVA POSE

Sammy says we lose balance in old age and, boy, is he right. At home, just thinking about getting up on a chair with a broom to clean the cobwebs makes me dizzy! I was never a *baleboste* like my sister Pearl, who lives to clean.

In Dancing Shiva Pose, you have to stand on one leg, like a flamingo.

Sammy likes to say, practice makes imperfect. I practice and practice wherever I am. At the bank, at D'Agostinos, in Central Park. I stand on one leg and breathe. At my age, you can't wait until you find a yoga room to practice yoga.

"Take it off the mat," as they say! Practice in those fancy Blahnik shoes (I call them *Bialy* shoes).

Here I am—a Jewish Yogini flamingo!

Setting a New Intention

When you're married a long time, like I was, you do wonder which one will go first. Since I'm the one who is left, I've set a new intention: to honor my Harry's memory by dedicating my *asana* practice to him every day.

It's like lighting a *yortzeit* candle for him daily. My body is the dancing flame that continues to burn for him.

Vriksasana: Tree Pose

"What kind of tree are you?"

Sammy walks around, asking us this as we balance on one leg, our arms like tree branches reaching up toward the sky. It's all so poetic it gives me the goosebumps!

"I'm an apple tree!" I blurt out. "Yes, a ripe old apple tree in autumn!"

Lateness, Shmateness

Today we have a substitute teacher, as Sammy is in Hawaii (poor *bubeleh*) at a special yoga conference. They sure know how to pick swanky locations for their conferences, these yoga folks.

The substitute teacher is twenty minutes late, which is very discourteous in my book. She didn't even apologize, but arrogantly said, "Your patience is the real test of your yoga evolution." What the hell does that mean? I had so much baking to do for Rosh Hashanah that during meditation I visualized dropping a giant honey cake on her head!

I guess I'm not very evolved.

P.S. How we resist change! It's so easy to get attached—*azoy!* To a yoga teacher, even.

UTKATASANA: SEATED CHAIR POSE

Sammy has a wonderful sense of humor (similar to my own, I must say). When we are in Seated Chair Pose, he says, "Try to think of it more as a love seat than a bar stool!"

Then he comes over and gently presses down on my shoulders, so my *tush* will sink down into this seat of love.

I almost forget about the burn in my thighs.

Sethu Bandasana: Bridge Pose

Lots of back bends in class today. Bridge Pose is
supposed to stimulate your thymus, whatever that is.
Back bends are a natural antidepressant.

As I inhale, my *tush* up "toward the heavens," I have
a vision. I see the Brooklyn Bridge. Harry and I are
walking across it on a Sunday afternoon.

It is 1955, and we are dating.

I can still feel the warmth of his hand in mine.

The body never forgets.

WISHING FOR A KVETCHING CLUB

I overheard one woman talking about stress. She
could have stress? Her nanny calls in her nonfat
grande mocha lattes to Starbucks, for God's sake!
But at least she was *kvetching*.

You know what's wrong with yoga? They
haven't mastered the art of *kvetching*. The *kvetch*,
or complaint, is at the heart of *Yiddishkeit,* Jewish
culture. If you *kvetch,* you can at least let off steam,
make believe you have control over things that go
wrong. And I don't need to tell you that, historically
speaking, things haven't been so *gezunt* for the
Jewish people.

I feel like everyone's trying to be so damned happy
in yoga classes. Oprah has her gratitude journal,
which is fine. But we need a *kvetching* club!

At the top of my list? Why do people say to
me, "Ruthie, if it doesn't kill you, it makes you
stronger"? I'm strong enough, yet still weak with
grief. For me, a little *kvetching* is the aerobics for the
heart's longing.

KABBALAH AND YOGA

All this yoga has moved me to explore Judaism. I've enrolled in a course at the New School on *Kabbalah*. Maybe I'll run into Sandra Bernhard—I love that woman's *chutzpah*.

I've always been a firm believer in learning something new every day. I used to read the *Reader's Digest* "Improve Your Vocabulary" column religiously.

So what did I learn today?

Kabbalah means "reception," as Moses received the Torah from Sinai. Sammy says, "To enter *samadhi*—enlightenment—also requires us to be receptive. Reception is not passive; it's fully present and attentive to what is." Let me see if I got this right: Moses received the Torah, I receive "Sammy-dhi."

This is deep, what I'm saying. I sound like my New Age neighbor Maxine. Harry used to say she's in purge-atory, praying to the colonic God. She eats a steady diet of Anthony Robbins videos and frozen grapes.

MATSYASANA: FISH POSE

Fish Pose is so delicious to do after Shoulder Stand, considered the queen of poses. It opens up all the muscles in the shoulders and increases circulation to the neck, too. Oh, if my mother had only known about Fish Pose—she had such rounded shoulders!

In Fish Pose, I picture *gefilte* fish—and Harry wanting me to make it from scratch. Rokeach brand is the best, but you have to know how to doctor it up!

Then I realize I am having a conversation about *gefilte* fish with a dead man . . . while the rest of the class has moved on to Dolphin Pose.

Fahrklempt in Cobra

Bhujangasana, or Cobra Pose, strengthens the lower back. It's especially good for women since it tones the ovaries.

In Cobra Pose, all *I* can see is Adam and Eve—the snake tempting Eve with the apple, which makes me think of sin and the daily headlines. We humans are freed and burdened by the knowledge of good and evil. The world is a quilt of yin and yang—love and hate, earth and heaven, sadness and happiness.

If only it could be soothed by a dab of lavender oil. Or a human touch.

Ahimsa—Do No Harm

The yoga teaching today is on *ahimsa*, or nonharm.

Traditionally *ahimsa* meant "do not kill or hurt people." Just like in the Ten Commandments. We should have compassion toward ourselves and others. It means being kind and treating all things with care.

For instance, if I tried to put myself into *poorna dhanurasana*, the full Bow Pose, where you lie on your stomach and grab hold of your feet and lift your head—this would not only be a *meshugana* thing to do (for which I should have my head examined), but also an act of violence toward myself. I would be fighting my body, trying to contort it into a shape that it shouldn't be in. I would be forcing my body to change what it's saying. I'm fine just the way I am, thank you very much.

Sammy says, "Yoga is not about self-improvement; it's about self-acceptance." He teaches that violence and awareness cannot coexist. When we are forcing, we are not feeling. Conversely, when we are feeling, we cannot be forcing.

After class and all this talk about doing no harm, I began to feel guilty. I must admit, I've murdered a lot of insects in my day. If a mosquito keeps me up all night, I have to do something about it.

Once I caught a glimpse of myself in the mirror as I was standing on the bed, my hair in rollers, a rolled-up AARP magazine in hand, swatting at a damn mosquito.

"Many Paths, One Truth"
—Sri Swami Satchidananda

Many paths, many paths. Over five thousand
Hindu gods in the pantheon of gods—it's no
wonder whenever I drive I get lost. Even a Global
Positioning System doesn't help my *farmisht* head.
My daughter got me a custom-made GPS with Burt
Reynolds's voice: "Turn left, turn right. Go straight
ahead until you reach the Dunkin' Donuts."

And when Roger, the Indian owner, and his wife,
Conti, see me pull in, they prepare my glazed
doughnut and small coffee. They don't charge me
for the coffee. Real *mensch*. Hardworking folk.

Many paths, many generous people out there.

Roger always says, "The doughnuts, they are *kosher,*
Ruthie!"

I don't dare tell them how much I love a good BLT
sandwich now and then.

INCENSE

Would you believe I used to confuse the word *incense* with *incest?*

And when Stephie's mother would burn incense, I thought she was smoking pot! We were so naïve in those days.

These yoga teachers love to burn incense. Sometimes I wonder what smell they are trying to cover up. Is the world that smelly? Or just our yoga room?

Incense (and incest, for that matter) makes me nauseous. I think I may even be allergic to it. It makes my eyes burn. And some of those pregnant women doing yoga, how they don't throw up, I can't comprehend.

When I was pregnant with Stephie's mom, I had to stop wearing any perfume at all.

Harry said I smelled like a pregnant woman. What does a pregnant woman smell like?

"Hope," he said. He was very poetic, my Harry.

Tapas

Sammy was telling us about *tapas*. I thought he said, "topless," and all through class, I pictured topless dancers saluting the sun.

Tapas does not refer to little Spanish *noshes,* either. In yoga, *tapas* means to have a burning zeal in practice, to be enthusiastic for health. And by the way, the word "enthusiasm," it turns out, originally meant receiving the breath of God.

Sometimes I feel like the whole world is connected through words and the roots of words. *Tapas, topless, nebbish, blemish, yiddish, tuches, pulkes, gornisht, witch, Dorothy, wizard, blizzard.* A paradise of Babel, where we all understand each other perfectly!

Most of the time, I feel like we're all just kicking each other in the ass with our fancy words. You *nosh* on me and I *nosh* on you. A dog-eat–dog rat race. Or is that a Downward Dog rat race?

Personally *I* am enthusiastic about an Epsom salt bath to soak my aching arms. Topless.

Yoga of Dark Chocolate—
Pure Pleasure!

Is the body a temple or a machine? Are we divine creatures or mechanical beings—ring the bell and, like Pavlov's dogs, we jump.

I know one thing—I can't pass up bittersweet chocolate. Harry used to bring me Godiva chocolates on special occasions. One day he came home with some espresso truffles. What's the occasion? "It's some Catholic saint's day," he quipped.

Every day was a holiday—a holy day—with Harry.

Toxic, shmoxic—God wants my body to be a temple for chocolate.

MARICHYASANA: TWISTS

In my day there was a dance called the "twist." This
is altogether different. As you exhale, you turn, as if
looking over your shoulder. You try to sit up tall—
no slumping! I renamed it the *dreyen asana*—since
dreyen means to turn or twist.

It's supposed to be like "a spring-cleaning for your
internal organs." My gallbladder didn't thank me.
Every time I exhaled I felt like my *kishkes* were
going to rupture!

One *nudnik* in class asked if we were allowed to
close our eyes during this *asana*. I had to lay my *own*
eyes on this voice with no *sechel*, no common sense,
for who asks such a question?

I turned around so fast, God punished me.
Boom—I heard something stretch a little too far.
Pooh, pooh, pooh, it shouldn't be fatal.

This time, my intercostal muscles—I didn't know
I had them—are going to soak in an Epsom bath.
Who needs this *tsuris,* this trouble?

SOLAR PLEXUS

Today was devoted to building our core strength,
without which you can't do anything. I don't know
how I've survived. Isn't that Pilates territory, I asked?
A *shiksa*, a striking blonde, in the front row, with her
pupik all dressed up with rings, laughed out loud. It
made me see belly-button rings in a whole new light.

We did five rounds of rigorous *kapalabhati* breathing.
Then we did Dancing Eagle Crunches. You lie down
on your back and lift your legs up into the air. Next,
you wrap one leg around the other—wait, I'm only
getting started! Then you wrap one arm over the other.
(There's an order to all this, but who can remember?)
You pause, then find your center line. (Apparently
there's a *nadi* where all the *chakras* throw a party that
runs through the center of your body.) You find it in
order to stay focused. Now you are ready to crunch.

Between the *kapalabhati* breathing and the Dancing
Eagle Crunches, I felt like I was going to *plotz*.

Afterwards, Sammy asked what we learned from
this experience. I learned: better not to have a bagel
and lox before class.

UTKATA KONASANA: GODDESS POSE

In Goddess Pose you look like you're doing a jumping jack, but you're frozen with your feet apart and your arms over your head. It reminds me of Leonardo da Vinci's drawing *The Measure of Man* (or in this case, *Woman*).

Sammy said we can all be goddesses in this pose— even the men! I'm a *shaine* Jewish Goddess!

I weighed myself. Even though I have a little red wine with dinner these days, I am ten pounds thinner than when I began yoga about six months ago. I have more *koyech*—strength—than I've had in years. *Mazel tov* to me.

I think I'll treat myself to some *kugel* from Zabar's this *Shabbat*.

USTRASANA: CAMEL POSE

Sammy demonstrates *ustrasana*, Camel Pose. Just watching him, I get a pain in my back.

Looking at his body bending back as he grabs hold of his heels and lifts his heart up, I can't help wonder why this pose is called "Camel." This led me to wonder why Eagle Pose is called "Eagle," and why Crow is called "Crow." Sammy certainly did not look like a camel.

He explains that each *asana* corresponds to an emotional state. Back bends are about opening our hearts and being vulnerable. But I still wanted to know why it's called "Camel."

"Will the Camel Pose give me a hump like Ethel Schwartz's?" I ask.

The woman with the belly-button ring giggles. I wouldn't have expected her to giggle in such a high pitch. It made me re-evaluate blondes entirely. I never thought they had a sense of humor. My sister Pearl is a blonde, an out-of-the-bottle blonde, but still. And she doesn't even have a dry sense of humor.

When I did Camel Pose, I got thirsty. Maybe you become the camel?

I felt like I was in Israel, in the Negev.

GARUDASANA:
BRAIDED CHALLAH POSE

On my walk to yoga this morning, a bird pooped on my head. How do I know? When I got to the yoga center, someone said, "Ruthie, you have bird poop in your hair, dear." It just so happens we did *garudasana* today in class. This is translated as Eagle Pose, although Sammy says the name literally means "devourer," because Garuda was identified with the all-consuming fire of the sun's rays.

Garuda is a real pretzel of a pose. As I shift my weight onto my right leg (it's my stronger side) and wrap my left foot over my right thigh, and then wrap my right arm over my left arm, suddenly I feel like a braided *challah* loaf.

After class I stop at my favorite bakery and salute the wall of braided *challah* loaves, shiny with egg wash, sprinkled with poppy seeds. My body feels stretched and kneaded, like these beautiful loaves that will adorn *Shabbat* dinner tables. My old body feels like a new blessing.

Life is full of unexpected twists and turns—a sad, joyous braid. I started with the poop, which may have originated with an eagle, I moved to the Dancing Eagle (who knows—maybe the bird brought me luck?), and discovered miraculous loaves of bread. For the fun of it, I balance the *challah* on my head and make Jennifer, the bakery owner, laugh.

"Here, Ruthie, take another loaf on me."

Maya Boxes with God
on Coney Island

In yoga the idea of separation from the divine is considered an illusion, which they call *maya*.

I knew a woman named Maya who lived in Coney Island. She was from Russia and took long walks on the boardwalk every morning, no matter what the weather. And believe me, before this global warming, we had cold winters on the beach. But there was Maya striding with fierce purpose, pumping her arms through the wind as though she were fighting with the cold air, fighting with her own breath.

I would look out my window and think, *It looks like she's boxing with God.* Who knows what demons she was trying to walk off from the old country?

I thought of Maya today, on the Sabbath, in my sunrise morning class. Sammy was guiding us through a pretzel of a pose—*parivritta trikonasana* (Revolved Triangle Pose)—and he said, "Imagine it is easy, imagine it is easy."

Don't get me wrong, I'm not saying life is easy.
I'm just saying—like Jacob, who wrestled with the
Angel; like Maya, who walked the boardwalk; like
me, who comes to 6 a.m. yoga and contorts her old
body into triangles—we are all sweating our way to
eppes, something holy.

I'm boxing my way back to my beloved, but until
then, I'm going to try to imagine it's easy.

Virabhadrasana I: Warrior I

Sammy teaches that the warrior *asanas* are especially powerful for women.

As a Democratic activist, living with osteoporosis, having raised a family, and now taking on yoga, I think of myself as a very powerful, capable woman. *Eine shtark frau,* Harry always said. A strong woman.

So when Sammy says, "Don't be a worrier, be a warrior!" I breathe into that with my whole *neshome*, my whole soul.

I'm a Senior Citizen Power Warrior Bubby!

Virabhadrasana II: Warrior II

Sammy's words add a new dimension to familiar poses. In *virabhradasana II* he says: "Allow your gaze to settle over your front arm, which is the future. Your back arm represents the past. But you reside in the center of the posture, in this very moment."

He comes over and adjusts my head, centering me in the present.

Harry, I realize how often I live in the past.

The Yoga of the Red Corvette

Sammy read this in class:

> "The physical body can be compared to an automobile. To run a motorcar we need gas, electric current to ignite it, a cooling system, lubrication, and an intelligent driver to control its movements."
>
> —SWAMI VISHNU-DEVANANDA

My mind drifted like Noah's ark. Suddenly I'm with Harry in our 1976 mint-green Cadillac, driving to Niagara Falls. Oh, he was so proud of that car. My sister Pearl called it the pimpmobile. (They never got along.)

If my old body were a car, what kind of car would I be? A white Rolls-Royce? Too stuffy. A pink Cadillac? Too Mary Kay.

To be honest, with all this yoga, this old body purrs like a red Corvette.

Niagara Falls and Lubrication

I've always been a daydreamer. I'm in Crocodile Pose on the floor on my stomach, but in my heart I'm with Harry, driving to Niagara Falls. I can hear the waterfall rushing down, or is it the sound of *ujjayi* breathing in the yoga room?

Waves of water fill the yoga room. I feel like I have to pee.

When we drove, Harry always rested his hand on my lap.

Suddenly I feel a hand pressing on my back. It is Sammy adjusting my *asana.*

My dreamy mind was caught between Niagara Falls and Crocodile Pose. What did Sammy say about cars and bodies? My car needs lubrication!

Om and Amen

Sammy pointed out that the Sanskrit *Om* and the Hebrew *Amen* bear a remarkable resemblance. When you chant *Om* and press your lips together at the end, you can feel the vibrations reverberate through your heart.

Something's changing inside me. We chanted for an extra long time today in honor of the spring solstice.

Ommmmmmmmmm.

Ommmmmmmmmm.

Ommmmmmmmmm.

It was as though Harry were giving me his blessing.

"It's time, Ruthie. What did we always say? That life is for the living. Where there is breath, there is life. You are still a vital woman, *meine liebe*—my love—so beautiful and lithe. Go. Ruthie. Go find a man. Go live, my love. *Amen*."

CONNECTING

After the warrior poses, I felt bold, so I signed myself up for an online dating service—JDate. Guess what the "J" stands for?

To be healthy and to be lucky—*gezunt und glik*. These are blessings. I wrote this in my profile.

I crossed my fingers and sent it into the mysterious world of online dating. *Oy.* I can't believe I'm doing this.

I keep learning new things about myself since I started yoga. Like there's this other Ruthie inside me. It reminds me of those Russian dolls Stephie had when she was little. One doll inside another, inside another, inside . . .

I told Sammy I was scared. He said, "That's a juicy place to be, Ruthie."

Moyel Making Mischief in Virtual Reality

A man named Herman answered my ad. He's a *moyel*—he performs circumcisions. He has a long beard. He said the nastiest things, things I can't repeat in polite company. Things about his private parts.

His *ponem* was not *mies*—it was quite handsome, actually. But his words, *oy,* they left a bitter taste in my mouth. What's more, he addressed me as *ketsele*, pussycat.

I haven't been in a *mikve*—a ritual bath—in years. But after reading his note, I felt like I wanted to dip myself in water for hours.

Dating Is Scary: On Courage and Control

Do you ever really know someone? From such a *haimish* face, such ugly words. Oh, how I worry about my Stephanie dating in college. But what are you going to do? Keep the kids locked up in a prison? If yoga has taught me anything, it's to give up a sense of control. To be less reactive and more responsive to the daily annoyances in our lives.

Did I want to call up my second cousin Hilda, whose ex-husband's first cousin has all kinds of connections, and have him give this *moyel* Herman a cut he wouldn't forget? Sure I did. With my small, ego-driven, angry, distracted monkey mind.

What did I do instead?

I took Sammy's Sunday night restorative class, and with my legs up against the wall, my varicose veins in a state of bliss, my diaphragmatic breathing steady as my beloved Harry's snores, I restrained myself from making that call to cousin Hilda.

The word *courage* comes from the French word *coeur*, "heart." Like the lion in *The Wizard of Oz*, I summoned my courage and, in the morning, logged back on to my dating account. I wasn't going to let one obscene *schmuck* ruin my chances of finding love.

Another Try at Connecting

Dear Yoga-Gram,

Let's do Bridge Pose together, a bridge between you and me. I don't do yoga—my daughter told me about Bridge Pose. You certainly look beautiful in your online picture. How flexible you are!

I am a retired schoolteacher, not a fancy man, but I'm open to trying new things. I love how gentle your eyes look. Are they green or blue? Whatever color, they sparkle.

Warm regards,
Walter Kirshbaum

The Yoga of Flirting

Shalom and *Namaste,* Walter!

Please call me Ruthie. Thanks for noticing my eyes—
they are green. Do you take my word for it, or would
you like to see for yourself?

I am not interested in a fancy man, but a kind man, who
is flexible in his heart.

Your daughter sounds quite knowledgeable about Bridge
Pose.

What color are your eyes? Your hat is covering them.

Fondly,
Ruthie

Walter Makes His Move:
Bridge Pose Worked Magic!

Shalom, Ruthie! Thanks for your speedy reply to my note.

I find your newfound passion for yoga so refreshing. Since my wife died, I have become the proud father of two Saint Bernards—Moe and Curly, named after the Three Stooges. I always loved animals and, in another life, would have been a veterinarian. But life has its own path for us, I think.

Anyway, I love to go walking around the city with Moe and Curly. I get stopped so often I barely make it to 14th Street! My daughter says they do Downward Dog beautifully! I would be honored if you would meet me on the Brooklyn Bridge at dusk this Saturday, Ruthie. I'll be the fellow with two Saint Bernards on a red leash.

Fondly,
Walter

It's a Date!

Hi, Walter,

I love animals, especially dogs. You'll have to tell me
if I pronounce it "dawgs," the way my granddaughter
Stephanie says I do. I love the Three Stooges, too! And
the Marx Brothers. Woody Allen . . . I can take or leave.
I mean a man doesn't marry his own stepdaughter, for
God's sake. But I do like that Larry David on HBO. He
was a writer for *Seinfeld,* which to me was *gornisht* on
top of *gornisht*—nothing on top of nothing. Stephie says,
"Bubby, that's what it's supposed to be—it's existential."
Existential, schmexistential. She's at Berkeley in college,
my Stephanie. What *naches,* delight, I get from that girl.

I should warn you, Walter, that I'm a talker. But I'm a
good listener, too.

I'll be the woman standing in Tree Pose with red hair
and red shoes. Only kidding! I won't stand in Tree
Pose—who could balance with high heels? Brooklyn
Bridge is my favorite bridge in NYC. I'll see you and
Moe and Curly at dusk.

Warmly,
Ruthie

Anahata: Heart Chakra

During meditation, Sammy says, "Breathe in love,
breathe out anything not contributing to your
highest sense of self, the self you're most in love
with."

He says to add a color to the heart chakra. I imagine
my heart green and breaking open like a bud. I
think I felt it stretch.

To think—at my age—growing pains!

Rocking and Hugging

After back bend *asanas*, the body needs to be stretched in the opposite direction. Yin and yang. So we hug our knees into our chest and rock from side to side.

This is the Happy Baby Pose, which reminds me of a Chinese dish, you know, like Happy Family, Buddha's Delight, or Triple Delight Pan-Fried Noodles.

Great for the kidneys, the lower back, and the root *chakra*, this Happy Baby Pose—a triple delight!

Urdhva Dhanurasana: Wheel Pose

I did a real back bend today for the first time since
fifth grade. It's designed to open the heart chakra. I
wish someone had taken a picture. I feel like I can
do anything now.

I walked home the long way. If Harry could have
seen me, like a schoolgirl! I almost turned to tell
him. Maybe that's what love and all this yoga do to
a person—make you ecstatic.

Letting Go

Apparently, we have to learn not to cling to
things. There are *yamas* in yogic teaching, which
are restraints. One of these is *aparigraha*, or
nongreediness. It is good to learn to let go of things,
to know you are not dependent on things to live a
whole life. There is freedom in this.

I let go of the wall today, during Tree Pose. It
reminded me of letting go of the wall once while
I was ice skating. The excitement, the fear, is
overwhelming!

When I came home, I walked straight to the closet
and emptied it of Harry's clothes.

Time for somebody else to enjoy them.

Love at First Sight: Karma and Bashert

It dawned on me this was a date. And I hadn't been on a date in fifty years. At least he chose good dusky lighting. Easy on the wrinkles.

I practiced my walking meditation on my trek to meet Walter on the Brooklyn Bridge. Breathe in, breathe out. But the butterflies in my belly were stubborn and refused to settle.

As the sun was setting over the East River, I could see two Saint Bernards on red leashes *schlepping* a distinguished-looking man. He had a smile on his face that stretched from ear to ear.

When he gave me his hand, the dogs got loose, and, oh, they jumped up on top of me, and I lost my balance, and my heel got caught in the grate. The tourists snapped pictures, and my freshly set hair blew in all directions.

I looked up towards the heavens towards *Hashem,* Harry, *Krishna,* at the rising crescent moon, and I began to laugh. When I looped my arm through

Walter's, it felt like we were resuming a long walk. Our rhythms matched, our footsteps, our breath.

The Yogis call this good *karma.* I call it *bashert,* fated.

A new beginning.

Vegetarian Potluck

Some people eat to live. Well, I live to eat! I've always been a *nosher* and sometimes a *fresser,* a glutton. Thank God, not a *shikker*, a drunk.

Our yoga center had the Spring Solstice Vegetarian Potluck Dinner tonight. Someone made the most delicious Indian soup called Mulligatawny. Well, a lightbulb went on in my *farmisht kopf*, and I thought, why not mix the best of both worlds! So when I came home, I pulled out my Jewish cookbooks and concocted: Mulligatawny Matzo Ball Soup.

Ruthie's Mulligatawny Matzo Ball Soup

P.S. The Tamil words milagu tannir *mean "pepper water," so be prepared for lots of peppery spice! My Harry would have loved this—he loved spicy foods.*

BROTH

4 to 5 cups vegetable stock (bouillon cubes may be used here)

Bring to a boil, and you can add carrots, parsnips, potatoes, garlic cloves.

TO MAKE MATZO BALLS

(I like them lighter, so I add the seltzer)

1 ½ tablespoons canola oil

3 eggs

½ cup matzo meal

1 teaspoon salt

⅛ teaspoon ground
   white pepper

2 tablespoons seltzer

Here's the Indian part:

Add 1 teaspoon ground turmeric

¼ teaspoon cayenne pepper

½ teaspoon ground cumin seeds

1 teaspoon ground
   coriander seeds

Combine oil and eggs in a mixing bowl.

Add the matzo meal, then the spices, and mix thoroughly.

Add seltzer and salt, to taste.

Cover the bowl with plastic wrap and refrigerate the batter for 30 minutes or more.

Bring 3 quarts of salted water to a boil. Form the dough into balls the size of walnuts and drop into the boiling water.

Cover. Lower the heat and simmer for 30 to 40 minutes.

Drain and place in soup, or cool and freeze for when you get a yen for Matzo Ball Mulligatawny.

Guten appetite.

Injured

My good *karma* has finally run its course. After almost a year of yoga, last night I pulled my left hip—the replacement side.

The yoga people called my sister Pearl, who I've barely spoken to over the past ten years. I know you're asking, why my sister, who I don't get along with, and not my own daughter. Paging Dr. Freud! It's a whole *megillah*—I don't even think Freud could analyze it.

How did they get my sister's number? Good question. Sammy says I must have unconsciously wanted to reconcile, since I put down her number to call "in case of medical emergency."

Pearl came and began to rub my hip like no time had passed at all. You know, it's a *mitzvah* of the highest order in Judaism to come to the aid of a sick person.

She's always had healing hands, my sister.

I didn't have the heart to tell her . . . it was the other hip.

Forgiveness

Dear Ruthie,

A sexy redhead. Smarter. Hipper. I always lived in the shadow of my baby sister. When you married Harry—who Momma had her eyes on for *me*—well, my heart broke. But the moment he laid his eyes on you that Friday night in June, I had no chance.

How I acted at your wedding—and then at other family events, until you put an end to it and shut me out of your life—was a shame. All those years lost.

But I am here not only because you are *mishpoche,* my sister, but because I never stopped loving you. To be at your bedside and help you heal is a joy. If you're lucky to get old enough, old rivalries begin to lose their sting.

You were always the one to try the newest and latest—you listened to Sinatra before anyone, had sex before me, and ate *treyf,* nonkosher food like shrimp, with the Italian *shiksas* down the block.

Although this new passion for the yoga is a little *narrishkeit,* you've always been up on the latest fad.

May you become whole again and back on the yoga mat stretching and *schvitzing*.

I hope you can find it in your heart to forgive me.

All my love,

Your *schvester*,
Pearl

InterBeing★

My hip injury has been the strangest gift. I know that when I was in Pigeon Pose on the day of my injury, I was more in my head than in my heart. There was a new *yogini* on the mat next to me—a stiff young thing—and I wanted to show her what an older woman could do.

Did someone say "ego"?

Over these past weeks I've had a lot of time to study and read. *Yoga* comes from the Sanskrit root word *yuj*—to "yoke." To connect body, mind, and spirit. Interestingly (I just love etymology!), the word *religion* comes from the Latin *religare*—to "re-connect." And who can forget Michelangelo's painting in the Sistine Chapel of God's hand giving life to Adam? When Harry and I saw that on our trip to Italy, he squeezed my hand tight.

All these thoughts jump through my head as Pearl lies beside me on the full-size bed Harry and I bought at Gimbels in 1963, the year Kennedy was shot. It's just like when we were kids and shared a bedroom.

When I wake up, she hands me a glass of orange juice and some homemade *mandel* bread, the Jewish version of Italian *biscotti*. She always was a marvelous baker.

We talk about Saul and Harry, the absent men in our lives. We talk about being widows. About our children—and their children. How it feels to be a grandmother. When she says it feels like she knows more people who are dead than alive, I know what she means.

We talk about how fragile the body is at any age. We talk like sisters, like old friends.

We re-member, forgetting old grudges. We re-connect.

---

* *InterBeing is a word coined by the Buddhist monk Thich Nhat Hanh to describe the interconnectedness of all things.*

MIRACLES

My hip heals so quickly the doctor says, "Ruthie, it's a miracle at any age. What have you been doing?"

I give him a guest pass to yoga.

If he comes, *that* will be the miracle!

THE UNEXPECTED DREAMER

I took Pearl to the 8 a.m. Gentle Yoga with Sammy.
I feel like I have a new lease on life. Pearl is resistant
to yoga, but she thought Sammy was a doll.

"He's too young for you, Ruthie."

She always was the family pragmatist.

I'm the dreamer, it turns out.

Multiple Paths to Enlightenment

Pearl, Sammy, and I went for lunch to a quaint
French bistro in the West Village.

Sammy says there are many paths to Enlightenment.
The Zen masters sit in *zazen* meditation for hours.
The Jewish kabbalists believe we all contain a spark
of the *shechinah,* which, by the way, is a feminine
Presence of God. My cousin Morty swears that
smoking a Cuban cigar in Miami Beach at sunset
is as close to God as he's ever come. He doesn't say
this in front of his wife, Hildy, of course.

Pearl was falling in love with the crème brûlée,
licking her lips and rolling her eyes.

I think I found one sure path to Nirvana:
watermelon martinis.

If God is in the details, I like the details of the
umbrella, the lime juice—and no pits!

SILENCE

A quiet room used to scare me. I liked the
background clutter of noise. Like during the
holidays, when everyone is talking all at once.

I know sometimes I drove Harry crazy with all my
chatter.

But now, I like the silence.

I like to listen to myself breathe.

Sirsasana: Upside Down

A surprise guest joined us for dessert (profiteroles: those are fancy cream puffs!). Sammy's partner of eight years, Greg. What a polite, handsome man, a lawyer.

It just so happens we did Headstand Pose in class today. Talk about turning the world upside down!

You never really know how far you can go. How thrilling it is to stand on my head, which I did today, with just a little help, for about two seconds.

What a different perspective. What freedom.

SAVASANA: CORPSE POSE

After all that *schvitzing*—sweating—finally, a
mechaye—a pleasure: we get to lie down and close
our eyes.

Sammy says this is a real pose . . . as long as we
don't fall asleep.

He explained that in this culture, we are in denial
of death. That is why, at the end of each yoga
class, we practice *savasana*—which (literally) means
"Corpse Pose." So we can practice living and dying
in a single breath.

Full acceptance. Peace and love. *Om Shanti* and *Om
Shalom*. They both mean "peace," one in Sanskrit,
the other in Hebrew.

And the beautiful thing is, it's all inside us.

GURUS IN THE CATSKILLS

I have signed up for the 200-level Yoga Teacher Training in the Catskills. It takes place at the same hotel where Harry and I used to vacation over the summers. I feel like I've come full circle.

Walter bought me a new yoga outfit for my venture. He says I have stretched his heart in ways he didn't think possible.

We are all each other's gurus, aren't we?

Gratitude for Stephie's Mitzvah

Stephanie, *shaine maidela,* are you there? Pick up. It's Bubby. I want to thank you for my yoga classes, *bubeleh.* It's been a year of bliss.

I can tickle the stars because you did a *mitzvah,* my granddaughter, by giving me this year of yoga—sometimes I can hear Zayde Harry *kvelling*—for both of us.

I didn't think an old Bubby like me could do this sort of thing, but here I am—seventy-three years young, and while I'm no *maven,* I can touch my toes!

You taught me not to be afraid to reach for the stars, my dear *maidela.*

Om Shalom.

Your Bubby,

Ruthie Brodstein,
aka Ruth Om Shalom

YIDDISH & YOGA
GLOSSARIES

Yiddish Glossary

AZOY So; thus. If you eat too many *bialys* before you do yoga, you will get a stomach ache—*azoy*.

BALEBOSTE A good homemaker, like my sister Pearl. You can eat off her kitchen floors. Harry used to complain she plugged in the vacuum cleaner while we were still having dessert and coffee.

BASHERT Destined or preordained, usually with reference to a romantic partner. Can you have more than one *bashert* in this life?

BIALY Short for *bialystoker,* from *Białystok*, a city in Poland. This is a small savory roll usually filled with diced onions, which is a traditional dish in Polish Ashkenazi cuisine and a close cousin to the popular bagel.

BIS HUNDERT UN TSVANTSIK You should live until 120; have a long life. This is what Stephanie wishes for her Bubby, so she gave me the gift of yoga.

BUBBY Grandmother. Affectionate term of endearment, the diminutive of *bubeleh*, used between a husband and wife, parent and child, or siblings. "My Stephie is my *bubeleh* and I'm her Bubby."

CATSKILLS An area in upstate New York where many a Jew spent summer vacations in hotels like the Concord. Now, many yoga *ashrams* make their homes there.

CHUTZPAH To have guts and courage; to be a little outrageous. A supermodel-type stuck her head into the lunchtime yoga class, rolled her mat out, looked at me, and said, "I didn't think this was the senior citizen class." What *chutzpah*.

DREYEN To spin or twist and turn, like when you do *marichyasana,* named after the sage Marichi, which incidentally means "ray of light."

EINE SHTARK FRAU A strong woman. Harry said this to me so many times, I think it sunk in.

EPPES This word has many meanings, depending on how you use it. It implies something is awry, off-kilter, or a complete mystery, as in "*Eppes,* this yoga room is so hot I'm going to faint!"

FAHRKLEMPT All choked up. Sometimes there are those days when I get all emotional.

FARMISHT All mixed up, which was how I was during my first few yoga classes.

FRESSER A glutton. My mother's brother, Jacob, was a *fresser*—he loved her pot roast so much he would take the whole serving plate as his own.

GEFILTE FISH Poached fish patties or balls made from a mixture of ground, deboned fish, usually carp or pike. I always bought the Rokeach brand and doctored it up, but my sister Pearl made it from scratch—that's why she's the *baleboste!*

GEZUNT UND GLIK Health and luck, the precious blessings I wish for everyone.

GORNISHT Nothing. That show *Seinfeld* seemed to be about *gornisht,* but Stephie explains to me that was the point. When did the point become nothing?

HAIMISH Homey or intimate. Sometimes you meet someone and they seem familiar; they remind you of home.

HANUKKAH The 8-day Jewish Festival of Lights, usually observed in late November or December, commemorating the rededication of the Holy Temple in Jerusalem in the 2nd Century.

HASHEM God. In Hebrew literally "the Name."

JDATE The "J" stands for Jewish. This is an Internet dating service where many contemporary Jewish (and non-Jewish!) men and women are finding their *basherts* (soulmates).

KEPELEH Head. This is how I remember *kapalabhati* breathing means "head breathing."

KISHKES Intestines, belly. To hit someone in the *kishkes* is to hit them in the guts.

KLEZMER A kind of music; in Hebrew, *kley* means a kind of instrument and *zemir* means song, hence *klezmer*. Lots of dance songs for weddings and other celebrations!

KNISH Potato dumpling.

KOSHER Orthodox Jews don't eat pork or shellfish and have certain dietary rules—they keep *kosher*. If something sounds suspicious you might say, "That doesn't sound *kosher*," as in "I saw Harriet Schwartzman at Zabar's Sunday walk past a sample of lox."

KOYECH Strength. I don't know where I find the *koyech* to hold Warrior I at 6:30 in the morning.

KUGEL A pudding made out of noodles or potatoes; deliciously fattening comfort food.

KVELL To take pride or great joy in something or someone, as I do in my granddaughter Stephanie.

KVETCH To complain, as in "If the yoga teacher doesn't arrive in five minutes, I'm leaving."

LATKES Rhymes with "vodka." These are potato pancakes that are traditionally eaten by Ashkenazi Jews during the Hanukkah festival celebrating the miracle of light. Think Indian *samosa* cooked in canola oil (not *ghee*). Stephanie loves to come over for my *latkes* with applesauce. Frankly, it's a miracle if the *latkes* don't fall apart while you're cooking them!

LOIF To run quickly, especially if you're trying to get to Loehmann's post-holiday sale.

MAIDELA A girl, like my granddaughter Stephanie. But since she goes to college where she studies women's studies and philosophy, she prefers I call her a young woman.

MANDEL Almond, as in *mandel* bread, the Jewish version of Italian *biscotti*.

MAVEN A really knowledgeable person. Sammy is a yoga *maven*. I'm a chocolate *maven*.

MAZEL TOV Good luck; congratulations. When I told Stephanie my injury wasn't so bad, she said, "*Mazel tov*," as in "Thank God."

MECHAYE A great joy or delight, or a relief. It was a *mechaye* to take an Epsom salt bath to soak my aching feet after today's yoga class.

MEGILLAH This has come to mean a long, often boring story, but originally described the book of Esther, which is read during the Purim holiday. If you're sitting on a plane with someone and they begin to get too chatty about their sciatica and food allergies, go ahead and say, "I don't need the whole *megillah!*"

MEINE LIEBE My love. Harry was my first love, and he's always in my heart.

MENSCH A human being; an upright, honorable, decent person. Sammy is a real *mensch*, and he says so am I. Okay, so we have a little mutual admiration society going on—who does it hurt?

MESHUGANA A crazy man; (also **MESHUGA)** wild or nuts. "How do you expect me to do these *meshugana* poses?"

MIES Ugly. This Herman character was more *mies* on the inside than the outside.

MIKVE The public ritual bath where Orthodox Jewish women go to regain purity after menstruation or childbirth. In the Hebrew Bible *mikve* literally means "a collection." After the incident with Herman, I didn't go to a *mikve* but I did go to a restorative yoga class.

MISHPOCHE Family, central to Jewish life. Sammy is now part of my new extended yoga family.

MITZVAH A good deed. My Stephie did a *mitzvah* by giving me this year of yoga.

MOYEL One who performs circumcisions. I personally have trouble watching this ritual up close, so I stand in the back by the food and *nosh*.

NACHES Pleasure or satisfaction. I have much *naches* knowing Stephanie is happy and healthy. I also have begun to take pleasure in my own body for the first time in a long time.

NARRISHKEIT Foolishness, as in that show *Seinfeld*, which I think is about nothing, but my granddaughter Stephanie tells me that's the point. Then again, my sister Pearl thinks my newfound passion for yoga is a *narrishkeit*. To each her own *narrishkeit*.

NEBBISH A timid person; rhymes with "blemish" and "Yiddish."

NESHOME Soul. I try to bring my whole self to the yoga mat— body, mind, and spirit, or *neshome*.

NOSH A snack, which I was looking for on my first day of yoga class. I love to *nosh* on a good prune Danish and a cup of coffee, but not before yoga, as it repeats on me.

NUDNIK A boorish type of person, like some yoga teachers who play too much New Age muzak for my taste.

OY VEY Literally, "Oh, it hurts," but it can be used to express surprise, as in "*Oy vey,* this Tree Pose is challenging my legs!"

OY VEY IZ MIR Literally, "Oh, woe's me."

PLOTZ Literally, "to explode," like when Sammy played Louis Armstrong in class and I was going to burst with excitement.

PONEM Face.

PULKES Thighs.

PUPIK Belly button. Since I started yoga classes, I've seen so many *pupiks* with rings and beads. So festive.

RACHMONES Compassion or pity lies at the heart of Jewish thought. God is often called the God of mercy and compassion. And what's more, the Hebrew root *rekhem* means "a mother's womb." The rabbis taught that a Jew should treat others the way a mother feels for her unborn child. Sammy shows me an abundance of *rachmones* during yoga, always doting on me like a mother hen.

SCHLEP To drag or pull, like Walter's dogs, Curly and Moe, did to him on the Brooklyn Bridge. They *schlepped* him across the bridge to meet me!

SCHMUCK Literally, this means "uncircumcised penis," but in common usage it has come to mean an obnoxious person, as in, "That man was such a *schmuck* to push his way through the subway."

SCHVESTER Sister.

SCHVITZ To sweat, which I do in Sammy's classes. Helps me stay svelte!

SECHEL Common sense.

SHABBAT The Sabbath, Saturday, when observant Jews go to synagogue, and nonobservant Jews might do a yoga class and eat some *kugel* for breakfast.

SHAINE Pretty, like my granddaughter Stephanie. Rhymes with "rain."

SHAINE MAIDELA A beautiful girl, like my granddaughter Stephanie. Just look at her in those yoga poses—I am so proud of her.

SHALOM "Peace" in Hebrew; also a greeting, as in "*Shalom*, how are you?"

SHECHINAH The presence of God, associated with feminine energy. In Hebrew the word refers to a dwelling or settling of divine presence. You can feel the spirit in the yoga room when we're all breathing and sweating and inter-being!

SHIKKER One who likes to overindulge with alcohol—okay, a drunk. I myself never developed a taste for it other than a nip of Slivovitz on New Year's Eve.

SHIKSA A gentile girl or woman; you know, the kind Woody Allen and Philip Roth fall for, with blonde hair, blue eyes, scuba diver.

SIMCHA Party, joyous occasion, event.

TIKKUN HA-OLAM To save the world.

TREYF When something is not *kosher* and is forbidden, like shrimp or bacon.

TSURIS Suffering or problems. Oh, did I have *tsuris* when I lost my Harry, but tell me, who doesn't suffer in this life?

TUSH (TUCHES) Derriere, rear end. You have to lift your *tush* up to the heavens in Downward Dog.

YIDDISHKEIT Jewishness; Jewish culture.

YORTZEIT This is the anniversary of someone's death in Judaism, when you say special prayers in temple or at home, and light a special remembrance candle that burns for 24 hours.

ZAFTIG To have a little something to hold on to, as my Harry used to say; to be a little plump.

ZAYDE Grandfather. When my husband Harry died, Stephanie, my granddaughter, lost her *zayde*.

Sanskrit/Yoga Glossary

ADHO MUKHA SVANASANA Downward Dog Pose. For an older dog, I sure have learned new tricks. Make sure you're making the letter V-shape in this inversion. (If you pick up your leg, it's called the Fire Hydrant Pose.)

AHIMSA Nonharm. In addition to being a physical practice, yoga has dos and don'ts, like the Ten Commandments. Thou shalt not do any harm. I like to think of this as Indian *mitzvahs!*

ANAHATA CHAKRA Heart center. It's associated with the color green, like my eyes. This energy center deals with love and openness, devotion, forgiveness, and joy. During meditation, Sammy tells us to place our hand on our heart and ask our heart how it's doing today.

APARIGRAHA This is one of the *yamas*, or rules of conduct, in yoga. The *yamas* are the "thou shall nots" of yoga (as in the Ten Commandments in the Hebrew Bible) and the *niyamas* are the "thou shalls." *Aparigraha* means nonhoarding, to receive the right amount. I think of it as the three bears approach to life—not too much, not too little.

ASANA Yoga posture. According to the Yoga Sutra, the first codification of yoga (which dates back about 2,000 years), each *asana* should have the qualities of alertness and relaxation. When no effort is necessary, you can relax and let go completely. Only 3 of the 196 aphorisms in the Yoga Sutra refer to physical postures, so do the postures with a calm, focused mind.

BHUJANGASANA Cobra Pose, which is great for strengthening your lower back and massaging your abdomen. I have to confess, sometimes if I'm feeling grumpy, I hiss like a snake when I'm in this pose. No one's perfect.

BRAHMAN The principle of unity in Hinduism.

CHAKRA Energy center.

DHYĀNA Meditating.

GARUDASANA Eagle Pose or, for me, Braided Challah Pose! Great for developing concentration and coordination. Great to go home and tear off a piece of warm *challah*. Releases tension in my shoulders to eat warm bread on a cold winter night.

GURU Teacher. Sammy is my favorite guru. He tells me sometimes the people who give us the most trouble are often our best teachers. In that case, Ethel Schwartz, who I see on Friday mornings at the kosher bakery, must be my guru supreme, because she always forgets to take a number and then cuts in line in front of me. *Oy!*

KAPALABHATI Bellow-like breathing. *Kapala* means "skull" in Sanskrit.

KARMA Action, duty. Sammy says I have good *karma*.

KARMA YOGA The yoga of service; doing good deeds, with no strings attached.

KRISHNA A deity in Hinduism who takes on different guises: he can be a god-child, a prankster, a lover. In case you are watching *Jeopardy*, the Sanskrit word *krishna* literally means "black," "dark," or "dark blue."

MANTRA A chant. As in *Om Nama Shivaya*, or *Baruch Ata Adonai*, or *Gefilte Fish Oy My-a*.

MARICHYASANA Twisting Pose. Named after the sage Marichi, which incidentally means "ray of light."

MATSYASANA Fish Pose.

MONKEY MIND A Buddhist term to describe the mind in a distracted state, jumping from branch to branch of the Bodhi tree.

Never judge your monkey mind harshly. Just watch yourself jump around and try to be compassionate with yourself.

MUDRAS Hand gestures or "seal," used as an aid to meditation. Hands are so expressive, when you watch Indian dance, the *mudras* are exquisite and tell a story.

NADI The yogis believe there are many thousands of *nadis*—energy meridians—in our bodies. The largest is called the *sushumna nadi* and runs from the base of the spine to the top of the neck. I like to think I have this mysterious *kundalini*, serpentine energy that runs through the center of my body that I'm trying to uncoil.

NAMASTE "The light in me honors the light in you." Stephanie said in L.A., when they reject you from a fancy schmancy restaurant, the yoga-body hostess will bring her hands together in a reverential *namaste* gesture, and it makes Stephie hiss (maybe she got the hissing tendency from me, *oy*). *Namas* means "to bow" and *te* means "to you." Sammy ends class by saying *namaste*.

NATARAJASANA Dancing Shiva Pose, or Lord of the Dance Pose. A stunning balancing pose where you hold one foot behind you, lift your heart, and shine.

OM NAMA SHIVAYA A popular mantra to the goddess Shiva.

OM SHANTI Peace. We say it three times at the end of class. And sometimes, Sammy looks at me and adds, "*Om Shalom,*" since *Shalom* means "peace" in Hebrew. So many connections.

PARIVRITTA TRIKONASANA Revolved Triangle Pose. Beginners, please get your blocks for this one, or you'll fall right on your *tush*. This one is full of twists and bends and spinal extensions—an advanced, delicious pose to be done with care.

POORNA DHANURASANA This is also called *urdva chakrasana*, an advanced yoga pose, not to be done without exercising caution. You lie on your belly, grab your feet, and lift your legs into the shape of a bow. My yoga is to watch someone else do it and inhale their good *karma*.

PRANA Breath. At first, I thought, why do we have to learn how to breathe—it's one thing I can do without thinking. Boy, did I have a lot to learn!

SAMADHI Enlightenment, the final stage in the yogic path. Also called Nirvana, Heaven, Bliss, a good prune Danish and a hot cup of coffee!

SAVASANA Literally, "Corpse Pose," but not morbid at all. Try it, you'll like it. It's a *mitzvah* after all that stretching.

SETHU BANDASANA Bridge Pose. Compare my Bridge Pose to my granddaughter's and you can begin to appreciate the variety of poses and possibilities in yoga!

SIMHASANA Lion Claw Pose.

SIRSASANA Headstand Pose. I did it for two seconds and it literally turned my world upside down!

SURYA NAMASKAR Sun Salutes. Imagine waking up and being so grateful for a new day, you bow to the sun in humility. I love my "sun-dances." When I link movement with breath, I'm in the flow of life.

TAPAS To build heat in the body; zeal for practice. Not to be mistaken for the delicious Spanish *noshes* called *tapas*.

UJJAYI Throat breathing, or ocean breathing. If you go to an *ashtanga* class, the *ujjayi* breathing is so powerful it feels like the room is breathing in and out.

URDHVA DHANURASANA Upward Facing Bow Pose, or Wheel Pose (also called *chakrasana*). This one takes practice, but with persistence and open shoulders, you can do it. If you have a slipped disk, stay away from it and visualize yourself doing it instead.

USTRASANA Camel Pose. The last time I saw a live camel, I was in Israel.

UTKATA KONASANA Goddess Pose. Looks like Leonardo da Vinci's *The Measure of Man* sketch, where you stand in a sort of jumping jack, with all your limbs outstretched, and breathe deeply into your solar plexus. Some folks like to do this lying down, which is relaxing.

UTKATASANA Seated Chair Pose, or Fierce Pose. You can sink into a love seat and get a real burn in your thighs, or you can be less fierce, but no less yogic, and just dip into a bar stool. Not that I know what a bar stool would feel like; I haven't been to a bar since my cousin Morty's daughter was married to a Protestant man and they had an open bar at the wedding. I got a little *shikker* on apricot sours.

UTTANASANA Intense forward stretch. Whenever we bow forward, we are taught it's an act of humility and grace—how can you not love that idea?

VINYASA YOGA Breath synchronized with movement, a flowing style of yoga that makes me feel like I'm dancing!

VIRABHADRASANA I AND II Warrior Poses. I am a Fierce Warrior Yoga Bubby!

VRIKSASANA Tree Pose. *Vriksa* means "tree." This is a balance pose where you stand on one leg, focus your *drishti* (gaze) on one spot that won't move (not a fly, like I saw one gentleman do once and when it flew away, he tipped over), and breathe. What kind of tree are you? A mimosa, an apple? I was a weeping willow, and now I am an apple tree!

YOGA From the Sanskrit root word *yuj*, to unite, yoke, or join body, mind, and breath.

ACKNOWLEDGMENTS

Thanks to: Phil Halpern for the support and encouragement that made me write this book; Jean Marie Courtney, yoga student extraordinaire; Susan Golding for her *sechel* in all things; Judy Jacobson for her Yiddish insights; Sherri Edelman, Jane Freeman, Kelly Gallagher, and Sylvia Boorstein for their generous support; Ilene Beckerman for taking the time; Kate Epstein for her initial belief in Yiddish Yoga; Mimi Schwartz for the introduction; Diana Cavallo and Bernard Stehle for pushing me harder; and Art Glazer for his witty, whimsical illustrations. A special thanks to Robert Margolis for his love and devotion to Ruthie and to me.

I am indebted to Heidi Sachner, Keith Holla-man, Harry Burton, and the staff at Newmarket Press, not only for their immense skills and talents, but for their kindness and generosity. I am honored to know such *mensch*. Finally, thanks to Esther Margolis, without whose guidance, keen reading eye, and gracious support this book simply would not be.

About the Author

Lisa Grunberger holds a Ph.D. in Comparative Religions from the University of Chicago Divinity School and teaches writing in the English department at Temple University in Philadelphia. She has taught yoga for many years, and is also a published poet and performer.

A native New Yorker from Long Island who grew up with an Israeli mother and a Viennese father, Lisa was immersed in *Yiddishkeit* from a young age. *Yiddish Yoga* is her first book.